MEDITATIONS FOR MARITAL INTIMACY

SPIRITUAL REFLECTIONS FOR SEXUAL ENRICHMENT AND ONENESS IN MARRIAGE

A resource like this to help couples have better and more open discussions about their intimate relationship is enthusiastically welcomed and so needed. Especially in bringing the power of gospel principles into the intimate sexual relationship, these meditations will help husbands and wives better understand divine sexuality and advance concepts and questions they didn't even know to talk about in the first place.

—**Laura Brotherson, LMFT, CST, Author of** *And They Were Not Ashamed* **and** *Knowing Her Intimately*

These meditations, if practiced with a sincere desire to deepen understanding, will truly transform not only how you think about the essential facts of your life but, more importantly, how you will see and cherish your partner. They will deepen your connection, help you stand the test of time, and prepare your coupling for eternity. This isn't just a book you must read—this is a book you must talk about and make a habit.

—**Dr. Matt Townsend, Author of** *Starved Stuff: Feeding the 7 Basic Needs of Healthy Relationships*

Read every page! *Meditations for Marital Intimacy* is a treasure trove of knowledge, and the questions are illuminating.

—**Jonathan Decker, Your Family Expert**

Meditations for Marital Intimacy is a wonderful way for husbands and wives to "check in" with each other and create meaningful, passionate intimacy.

—**Michael Goodman, Associate Professor of Church History and Doctrine, Brigham Young University**

The ponderables in this book help get the answers to the hard-to-ask questions!

—**Meg Johnson, Author and speaker**

Meditations for Marital Intimacy is an excellent resource.

—**Dean M. Busby, Professor, School of Family Life, Brigham Young University, Coauthor of** *Sexual Wholeness in Marriage*

MEDITATIONS FOR MARITAL INTIMACY

SPIRITUAL REFLECTIONS FOR SEXUAL ENRICHMENT AND ONENESS IN MARRIAGE

JENNILYN AND DAVE YOUNG

Copyright © 2020 by Jennilyn F. and Dave F. Young. All rights reserved.

Original artwork: Katie Sumsion

Photo credit: Lisa Moore, @lisamoorephotography

Disclaimer

This material is neither made, provided, approved, nor endorsed by Intellectual Reserve, Inc. or The Church of Jesus Christ of Latter-day Saints. Any content or opinions expressed, implied, or included in or with the material are solely those of the owner and not those of Intellectual Reserve, Inc. or The Church of Jesus Christ of Latter-day Saints.

Permissions

President Kimball Speaks Out (1981), 2. © Deseret Book Company. Used by permission.
The Teachings of Spencer W. Kimball (1982), 312. © Deseret Book Company. Used by permission.
The Teachings of Ezra Taft Benson (1988), 409. © Deseret Book Company. Used by permission.
Joseph F. Smith, *Gospel Doctrine* (1939), 272. © Deseret Book Company. Used by permission.
Teachings of Gordon B. Hinckley (1997), 209. © Deseret Book Company. Used by permission.
Joe J. Christensen, *One Step at a Time: Building a Better Marriage, Family, and You* (1996), 39. © Deseret Book Company. Used by permission.
Robert L. Millet, *The Mormon Faith: A New Look at Christianity* (1998), 71. © Deseret Book Company. Used by permission.

Ellipses present in the source material are shown unbracketed; any ellipses inserted by the authors of this work are placed in brackets.

All biblical references are from the King James Version.

Cover designed by Angela Baxter
Edited by Haley Miller Swan
Typeset by Emily Chambers and Kaitlin Barwick

Printed in the United States of America

ISBN: 978-0-9907745-3-2 (paperback)
ISBN: 978-0-9907745-4-9 (ebook)

To husbands and wives

When it comes to spiritual truth, how can we know that we are on the right path? One way is by asking the right questions—the kind that help us ponder our progress and evaluate how things are working.

              —President Dieter F. Uchtdorf

Questions are an indication of a further desire to learn, to add to those truths already in place in our testimonies, and to be better prepared to "press forward with a steadfastness in Christ."

              —Elder Ronald A. Rasband

By asking sincere questions and by seeking divine answers, we learn "line upon line, precept upon precept," as we increase in knowledge and wisdom.

              —Elder Larry S. Kacher

CONTENTS

FOREWORD — XIII

ACKNOWLEDGMENTS — XVI

INTRODUCTION — 1

MEDITATIONS — 7

1. The Importance of Your Union — 9
2. A Divine Nature and Destiny — 10
3. Cleave to Each Other — 12
4. Perfect Love — 13
5. The Key to Happiness — 14
6. Sex Within Marriage Is Sanctioned by God — 16
7. Unload the Baggage — 18
8. Sexuality Comes from God — 20
9. Sex Within Marriage Is Sanctifying — 21
10. Sex Within Marriage Is Encouraged — 22
11. The Laws and Blessings of Marriage and Sexuality — 24
12. The Law of the Harvest — 25
13. Marital Priorities — 26
14. Our Bodies Are Sacred — 28
15. Our Bodies Are Beautiful — 30
16. Bridle All Your Passions — 31
17. Meaningful Touch — 32

18.	A Symbol of Total Union	34
19.	The Purposes of Sexuality	36
20.	Husbands and Wives Are Better Together	37
21.	Celestial Marriage Is Essential to Exaltation	38
22.	Love Each Other	40
23.	Giving and Receiving	42
24.	Enjoy Your Love Together	44
25.	Higher Thoughts	45
26.	Worldly Sex Versus Marital Intimacy	46
27.	Courteous Communication	48
28.	Seek First to Understand	50
29.	Mutual Acceptability	52
30.	A Part of Life with No Equal	53
31.	Be Fully Present	54
32.	The Choice Is Yours	56
33.	Be Humble and Acknowledge Your Faults	58
34.	Frequent Forgiveness	60
35.	Sincere Devotion	61
36.	Marriage and Sexuality as Divine Gifts	62
37.	The Significance of Biblical Terms	64
38.	Keep Christ as Your Center	66
39.	The Source of Lasting Fulfillment	68
40.	The Verity of the Covenant	70
41.	The Joy of Marital Intimacy	72
42.	Regular Rituals	73
43.	The Power of Patterns	74

44. The Power of Love	76
45. The Power of Gratitude	79
46. The Power of the Word	80
47. The Power of Prayer and Fasting	82
48. The Power of Faith	84
49. The Power of the Priesthood	86
50. Share Feelings	88
51. Practice Self-Care	90
52. Accommodate Life's Rhythms	92
53. Labor Together in Love	94
54. Counsel Together Regularly	96
55. Principles of a Successful Marriage	97
56. There Could Not Be a Happier People	98
57. The Marriage Metaphor	100
58. Love Is a Fragile Thing	102
59. When Troubles Come	104
60. Continue Searching for Truth	106
ABOUT THE AUTHORS	109
NOTES	111

Foreword

One of the most valuable gifts we can give another person is our full attention, or in other words, our complete presence. Being fully attentive and aware of another can be healing and nourishing. In a marriage, it can make the difference between a mediocre or a vibrant marriage. Unfortunately, our culture gives very little attention to being present in the moment. Instead we are bombarded with ways to be more efficient, and we celebrate those who can double and triple task. We eat while listening to music or watching TV. We constantly interrupt conversations because of a buzz or ding from our pocket or bag. We struggle to be without our devices and "disconnect" from the world. Yet, the connections that mean the most are neglected because we are "connected" to distraction. Struggling with divided attention is not a new problem, but it is a solvable problem.

Taking time to slow our thoughts, waking up to the details of our relationship, pondering the meanings behind the routine, sitting with the discomfort of our neglect, embracing the range of unfelt or felt emotion, and sharing these experiences with a loved, but sometimes distant, spouse is renewing, healing, and transformative.

Recent research has explored the value of being more attuned and less judgmental with ourself and our partner within a romantic relationship[1] and our sexual relationship.[2,3] These two skills seem simple, but they take practice and patience to develop. The meditations

---

1. J. G. Kimmes, M. E. Jaurequi, R. W. May, S. Srivastava, and F. D. Fincham, "Mindfulness in the Context of Romantic Relationships: Initial Development and Validation of the Relationship Mindfulness Measure." *Journal of Marital and Family Therapy* 44 no. 4 (October 2018): 575–89.
2. C. E. Leavitt, E. S. Lefkowitz, and E. A. Waterman, "The role of sexual mindfulness in sexual wellbeing, Relational wellbeing, and self-esteem." *Journal of Sex & Marital Therapy* 45 no. 6 (2019): 497–509.
3. C. E. Leavitt, E. S. Lefkowitz, Y. Akyil, and K. Serduk, "A Cross-Cultural Study of Midlife Relational and Sexual Health: Comparing Ukraine to the US and Turkey." *Sexuality & Culture* (2019): 1–22.

within this book may be particularly useful in encouraging couples to slow down, find meaning, share observations, and connect at a more authentic level of intimacy.

We should not underestimate the importance of a loving sexual relationship within a committed, striving marriage. Marriage is the vehicle that challenges us as individuals to face the errors in our own thinking, strengthen our functioning, broaden our perspective, and find meaning in loving endurance.[4] Consequently, giving useful tools to help couples create strong, lasting bonds is critical. We can use all the helpful tools we can get, and this book is one of those useful tools.

Just as sex should avoid an agenda but instead be a time of connection and awareness of our physical and emotional experience, this book allows the reader to take a number of topics in digestible pieces. Read a thought a week and ponder it. Read a thought daily with your spouse and discuss it. Read it all at once or on an as-needed basis. This book is a tool that can be referred to over and over.

During an interview, Mother Teresa was asked what she said to God when she prayed. "I don't say anything. I just listen," she explained. The follow-up question was, "What does God say to you?" Mother Teresa again explained, "He doesn't say anything. He just listens, and if you don't understand that, I can't explain it to you."

Do we understand the need to just be in the presence of God? Do we allow His Spirit to empower us and teach us what we do not know? Do we allow the peace of that divine relationship to infuse our marriage with peace and knowing? This God-given gift of sexual connection is intended to bond, unify, and create greater love and emotional intimacy—truly knowing the depths of a spouse.

Elder Holland spoke of sexual intimacy as the ability to give your everything—dreams, hopes, and sorrows.[5] We cannot give our everything to our beloved and receive their

---

4. David Schnarch, *Intimacy & Desire: Awaken the Passion in Your Relationship* (New York: Sterling Productions, 2009).
5. Jeffrey R. Holland, "Of Souls, Symbols, and Sacraments" (Brigham Young University devotional, Jan. 12, 1988), speeches.byu.edu.

everything if we are only partially aware of our own feelings and thoughts. We cannot give everything to our beloved if we are not attuned to their dreams, hopes, and sorrows. When we squeeze the artificiality out of our lives and stand vulnerable, yet strong, before our spouse, we are ready and able to give our everything.

Sex needs to be a comfortable conversation. When we talk openly about our sexual thoughts, disappointments, triumphs, and hopes, we take a step toward a stronger, more loving relationship. If this is not where your relationship is presently, take a step each day to move it in that direction. Satan has worked to distort sex in a number of ways.

Here are two common distortions: (1) sex is not sacred but instead common, to be shared with anyone, joked about, and used as a tool for personal pleasure, and (2) sex is shameful or embarrassing, a topic to avoid because it is at best awkward. Neither is true. Sex is divine. Intended to be shared within a committed, loving relationship, it is a means of strengthening and bonding couples and establishing unity within their interactions. Sex is healing, creative, empowering, and nourishing. It requires regular time and attention to be healthily maintained.

Meditations for Marital Intimacy provides readers with practical ideas for how to open up meaningful conversations about marriage, sex, intimacy, emotions, and all the ups and downs that go along with these topics. Regular chats about these intimate topics provide couples an opportunity to strengthen and unify their relationship. Enjoy!

Chelom E. Leavitt, JD/PhD

Assistant Professor, School of Family Life, Brigham Young University
Coauthor, *Sexual Wholeness in Marriage* and *A Better Way to Teach Kids about Sex*

Acknowledgments

We'd like to thank all those who have contributed to this work. We appreciate the thoughtful input from Cindi, Heather and Craig, Roger and Darlene, Mel and Joan, Jason and Andrea, Abe and Betsy, Steve and Adrianne, Carly and Chase, Rob and Jill, Ross and Kaye, and Karen and William. We'd also like to thank Katie Sumsion for her compelling line drawings.

We acknowledge the heaven-sent direction from Church leaders and their spouses that inspired and formed the core foundation of this book.

We are especially grateful for the beautiful marriages we have seen in our parents. Not only have John and Ilse Young and Jerry and Ann Fullmer been mentors, friends, and partners for us, but they have consistently modeled loving marriage relationships. Over the years, they have provided vivid examples of what husbands and wives do in lasting, happy marriages. Our marriage is better because of them.

Jennilyn and Dave Young

Introduction

The doctrine of eternal marriage is central to God's plan and essential to our eternal progression. We have found marriage to be our most rewarding relationship, while at the same time complex and soul stretching. Marriage offers the nourishing power of intimacy, including sexual intimacy. Yet, maintaining an intimate connection with your spouse doesn't always come naturally. We can't expect the nourishing magic of marriage to just happen. For us, even after twenty-nine years of marriage, connecting with each other is an ongoing process that often requires humility and understanding as we strive to become of one heart, one mind, and one flesh.

So much depends on a man and a woman becoming one. The family has been referred to as "the fundamental unit of society."[1] Strong families create strong communities, and strong communities are the building blocks of strong nations and societies. Stated in a religious context, a strong society is a Zion society. Strong families help us create the true at-one-ment of Zion.[2] If you want to build up Zion with strong and healthy families, the best place to start is with strong and healthy marriages. In order to create a strong marriage, there has to be a bonding connection, some intimacy, that ties that marriage together. Sexual intimacy is one of the best tools God has provided for married partners to strengthen and unite them as a couple.

Ironically, the very gift that God designed to connect and nourish married couples is often the cause of frustration and misunderstanding. Sexuality within marriage can be confusing, even for couples who have been married for decades. Otherwise healthy marriages can suffer from a lack of intimacy and the dangers of sexual dissatisfaction,

---

1. "The Family: A Proclamation to the World," *Ensign*, Nov. 2010, 129.
2. See "Living the Spirit of At-one-ment," in *Selected Writings of M. Catherine Thomas* (Salt Lake City: Deseret Book Company, 2000), 189.

including emotional emptiness, stress, contention, detachment, and even divorce. Some couples struggle being intimate at all. Other couples who are regularly intimate wear a path in those same grooves and find themselves asking what they can do to get to know their spouse more deeply. No matter where we are in our relationships, we could all benefit from more meaningful connections.

Both men and women need the nourishment that only true marital intimacy can give so they can strengthen their marriages and fortify their hearts in order to combat the strife that does and will attend us in the last days. Strong marriages are needed to help men and women weather these perilous times when men's hearts can fail them.[3]

How can we deepen our intimate connection? How can we make the most of our married sexual relationship? There are lots of questions about sex within marriage that need to be discussed and understood. Yet, even as married partners, we are often reluctant to talk about it. Of course, it is a sacred and personal topic, and we want to be respectful. But not talking about it is not the answer. If we never talk about married sexuality, we risk sending the message that it is undesirable, unimportant, or even sinful. On the other hand, talking about sex typically improves sex.

When sexuality is discussed in the Church, the conversation often centers around the dangers of immorality and the problems of pornography. These are important topics. But they aren't the whole story, particularly for married partners. Husbands and wives need more than the DON'Ts or the "Thou Shalt Nots." We often hear the negative side and nothing more. But there *is* more. Our married sexual education should include the DOs of sexual intimacy. It should include the "Thou Shalts" of sexuality for husbands and wives. Otherwise, we are living beneath our privileges. Getting that sexual education, with the answers that are unique to your relationship, is a process and challenge faced by every married couple.

---

3. See Doctrine and Covenants 45:26.

Our testimonies of the gospel assure us that God, as the creator of all things, is the author of sexuality. Thus, it makes sense that we turn to Him for answers on how to be better partners and better lovers. In addition, the Holy Ghost is always the best teacher. If we want to learn more about what President Nelson refers to as the "joy of true marital intimacy,"[4] it makes sense that we employ the same approach to learning about marital sexuality as we would for gaining knowledge about any other gospel truth. We turn to the doctrine of the gospel of Christ. For "the words of Christ will tell you all things what ye should do,"[5] and the Holy Ghost "will show unto you all things what ye should do."[6] Note that the scriptures say that the words of Christ will tell us *all* things, not just *some* things.

This may be what Elder Holland was trying to convey when he said, "The solutions to life's problems are always gospel solutions."[7] Heavenly Father wants us to succeed. He wants our marriages to succeed. He has promised us answers when we go to Him with a sincere heart and real intent.[8] In addition, when we exercise our faith, He helps us implement the solutions. Elder Holland continued, "Not only are *answers* found in Christ, but so is the power, the gift, the bestowal, the miracle of giving and receiving those answers. In this matter of love, no doctrine could be more encouraging to us than that."

Married partners looking for sexual enrichment may not naturally think about the principles of the gospel as a typical resource. But truth is not compartmentalized. On the contrary, the gospel embraces all morality and intelligence. And since all gospel truth is compatible, the truths about marriage and sexuality are puzzle pieces that fit and work together with all truth.

For example, the Word of Wisdom is a principle of the gospel. The blessings of living the Lord's law of health include the ability to run and not be weary and walk and not faint.

---

4. See Meditation 41, The Joy of Marital Intimacy.
5. 2 Nephi 32:3.
6. 2 Nephi 32:5.
7. Jeffrey R. Holland, "How Do I Love Thee?" (Brigham Young University devotional, Feb. 15, 2000), 2, speeches.byu.edu.
8. See Moroni 10:4.

At the same time, the physical body is one of the tools God has given to help connect us intimately as married partners.[9] If the Word of Wisdom is studied in respect to marriage, or in the light of being a better spouse, we may conclude that protecting and taking care of our bodies helps us be better marriage partners.[10] Perhaps this is one of the hidden treasures included in the blessings of obedience to this law.[11]

Another principle of the gospel is scripture study. When we study the Book of Mormon, for example, we don't typically do so with the expectation that simply reading it will improve our marriages. But, if you view the principle of scripture study in the light of marital relations, you can see how following this principle will bless your marriage.[12]

The exciting part is that we can get personalized, specific answers to the questions we each have to improve our own unique marriages. The purpose of sexuality, how to touch your spouse, how to receive the touch your spouse gives, what it means to be fully present with your spouse, and more, are all topics for which answers exist as part of the great whole of truth. The scriptures may not specifically spell out the answer. But like Joseph Smith, who asked a question prompted by scripture, each of us can receive the inspiration we're looking for by studying truth and pondering related questions.

With that in mind, we have compiled a selection of scriptures along with various statements from latter-day prophets and leaders that outline some of the doctrines, principles, and patterns for building strong marriages and improving intimate marriage relationships.

We have found that in addition to the scriptures and the words of modern prophets, a well-formed question often facilitates the deepest learning. It is the questions that stir the thinking, start the conversations, and reveal the clues that bring about the most precious discoveries. Following this same gospel study model, we've included questions

---

9. See Meditation 18, A Symbol of Total Union.
10. See Meditation 51, Practice Self-Care.
11. See Doctrine and Covenants 89:18–20.
12. See Meditation 46, The Power of the Word.

to help you make your own discoveries about marriage and intimacy. Even though this book poses questions, it is not a questionnaire. It is not a quiz. It has been said that if you want the right answers, you must ask the right questions. Just remember that every relationship is different, and it would be unreasonable to assume that one answer fits all. In relationships and spiritual matters, there is often more than one satisfying answer. In some cases, the answer itself may not even be the goal.

The gospel of Jesus Christ can be the best resource for strengthening your marriage as you study the principles, liken what you study to yourselves, search for applicable gospel truths, and listen for promptings from the Spirit. Personal revelation under the inspiration of the Holy Ghost is always our best source of truth. With that in mind, perhaps this book will act as a catalyst for that revelation as you and your spouse contemplate the significance of these truths and ponder their personal application. When you receive those promptings, record your thoughts and feelings and reflect on how best to apply the inspiration you receive.

Meditations for Marital Intimacy is for members of The Church of Jesus Christ of Latter-day Saints who are married, or who are about to be, who wish to further develop and better understand the blessings of marital intimacy, including sexual intimacy. It is different than most books on marriage and intimacy. While some resources aim to help couples with physical or emotional intimacy, *Meditations* can help a couple foster connection with a more complete or holistic approach because the principles included not only address physical and emotional intimacy but promote spiritual intimacy as well. Spiritual intimacy is created, in part, when husbands and wives have a mutual understanding of their roles in God's plan, the importance of their marriage in the eternities, and the blessings promised to husbands and wives who keep their marriage covenants.

Other resources address intimacy from an academic or clinical angle. You won't find relationship experts sharing personal anecdotes here. Neither will you find academics telling you what is considered to be normal with facts, figures, and footnotes. As valuable as these perspectives are, an approach taken by couples seeking their own solutions together through the study of doctrine and the influence of the Holy Ghost is unique and powerful.

We hope this compilation, along with the accompanying discussion questions, provides inspiration for husbands and wives everywhere who are looking to enhance their own intimate connection. At the very least, we hope this collection makes it easier for you, as married partners, to discuss not only your own relationship in general but also your sexual relationship, using the quotes and questions as a framework to begin and deepen conversations.

Remember that a marriage relationship is a living and ever-changing landscape that requires continual adjustment and attention. We grow, we age, we change, circumstances change, and our sexual relationship needs to change with it.[13] Just because a preference exists today doesn't mean it will be the same tomorrow. Married sexual interactions are therefore a process of continual discovery and evolution. Whether you're newly married or in a mature relationship, the doctrine and accompanying discussion questions can help you navigate that evolution. We hope that you use this as a resource that can be read and discussed over and over, because the questions and answers may be viewed and applied differently for you today than they might be a year from now, or five years from now, and so on throughout your married life.

Start where you are. Share what you can. Give and receive with love. The process of learning, asking, applying, and sharing is a pattern that will help you develop the intimate marriage relationship our Father in Heaven desires for you.

May the Lord's blessings be with you in your relationship as you seek to make the most of your marriage.

Jennilyn and Dave Young

---

13. See Meditation 52, Accommodate Life's Rhythms.

Meditations

The Importance of Your Union

Doctrine and Covenants 49:16
> Wherefore, it is lawful that he should have one wife, and they twain shall be one flesh, and all this that the earth might answer the end of its creation.

Spencer W. Kimball
> The earth cannot justify nor continue its life without marriage and the family. ("God Will Not Be Mocked," *Ensign*, Nov. 1974)

PONDER AND DISCUSS:

— Based on this scripture, for what purpose was the earth created?

— What are you doing in your marriage to become one flesh with your spouse?

— What areas in your marriage could benefit from greater oneness?

— What might happen if you fail to become one with your spouse?

— What is one way you would like your spouse to connect with you?

MEDITATION 1

A Divine Nature and Destiny

"The Family: A Proclamation to the World"

ALL HUMAN BEINGS—male and female—are created in the image of God. Each is a beloved spirit son or daughter of heavenly parents, and, as such, each has a divine nature and destiny. Gender is an essential characteristic of individual premortal, mortal, and eternal identity and purpose.

Sheri L. Dew

Satan seeks to confuse us about our stewardships and distinctive natures as men and women. He bombards us with bizarre messages about gender, marriage, family, and all male-female relationships. He would have us believe men and women are so alike that our unique gifts are not necessary, or so different we can never hope to understand each other. Neither is true. ("It Is Not Good for Man or Woman to Be Alone," *Ensign*, Nov. 2001)

PONDER AND DISCUSS:

— Why might the adversary want to confuse you about your roles as male and female, husband and wife, father and mother?

— How can learning about the differences in your divine nature, eternal identity, and purpose help you better understand and appreciate your spouse?

— How do you view your roles? Your spouse's roles?

— How are your roles complementary?

MEDITATION 2

- What is one thing your spouse can do to better support you in your roles?

- What is one thing you can do to better support your spouse in his/her roles?

NOTES _____

_____

_____

_____

_____

_____

_____

_____

_____

_____

MEDITATION 2

Cleave to Each Other

Doctrine and Covenants 42:22

Thou shalt love thy wife with all thy heart, and shalt cleave unto her and none else.

Mark 10:6–7

But from the beginning of the creation God made them male and female. For this cause shall a man leave his father and mother, and cleave to his wife.

PONDER AND DISCUSS:

- What does it mean to love your spouse with all your heart?
- What does "cleave" mean to you?
- Think of a time when you cleaved to each other with all your hearts. What is one thing you can do to generate that closeness more often?
- Why is it important to leave your father and mother and cleave to your spouse?
- Would your spouse say that you've appropriately left your father and mother?
- What and/or who might you be cleaving to more than your spouse? Are you willing to let it and/or them go in order to strengthen your marriage?
- What is one thing you can do to cleave to your spouse today?

MEDITATION 3

Perfect Love

1 John 4:18

There is no fear in love; but perfect love casteth out fear: because fear hath torment. He that feareth is not made perfect in love.

PONDER AND DISCUSS:

- What does perfect love look like to you?
- What is it about perfect love that dispels fear?
- What is one thing you can do to reduce any fear, anxiety, or insecurities you have about connecting with your spouse?
- What is one thing your spouse can do to minimize any fear, anxiety, or insecurities you have about connecting with him/her?
- What can you or your spouse do to reduce any fear, anxiety, or insecurities you may feel about your body?
- How can you overcome any fear you may feel about talking with your spouse about sex and sexual desire?
- What is one thing you can do to show love more perfectly?

MEDITATION 4

The Key to Happiness

Boyd K. Packer

The commandment to multiply and replenish the earth has never been rescinded. It is essential to the plan of redemption and is the source of human happiness. Through the righteous exercise of this power, we may come close to our Father in Heaven and experience a fulness of joy, even godhood. The power of procreation is not an incidental part of the plan; it is the plan of happiness; it is the key to happiness. ("The Plan of Happiness," *Ensign*, May 2015)

Within your body is the power to beget life, to share in creation. The only legitimate expression of that power is within the covenant of marriage. The worthy use of it is the very key to your happiness. ("To Young Women and Men," *Ensign*, May 1989)

PONDER AND DISCUSS:

— How might our sexuality be more than just an incidental part of God's plan?

— How has exercising the power of procreation brought you and your spouse closer together?

— How has the righteous exercise of the power of procreation brought you closer to our Father in Heaven?

— What might be a reason that sexual expression is legitimate only within the covenant of marriage?

MEDITATION 5

- How might the worthy use of your sexuality be the very key to your happiness?
- What is one thing you can do to utilize this key to bring more happiness to your marriage?

NOTES _____

_____

_____

_____

_____

_____

_____

_____

_____

_____

MEDITATION 5

Sex Within Marriage Is Sanctioned by God

Joseph F. Smith

The lawful association of the sexes is ordained of God, not only as the sole means of race perpetuation, but for the development of the higher faculties and nobler traits of human nature, which the love-inspired companionship of man and woman alone can insure. (*Teachings of Presidents of the Church: Joseph F. Smith* [Salt Lake City: The Church of Jesus Christ of Latter-day Saints, 1998], 158)

Spencer W. Kimball

In the context of lawful marriage, the intimacy of sexual relations is right and divinely approved. There is nothing unholy or degrading about sexuality in itself, for by that means men and women join in a process of creation and in an expression of love. (*President Kimball Speaks Out* [Salt Lake City: Deseret Book Company, 1981], 2)

PONDER AND DISCUSS:

— What are some of the purposes of our sexuality?

— How can you enhance your sexual intimacy as a genuine expression of love for your spouse?

— How might a marriage relationship be the most effective way to inspire mankind to develop the higher faculties and the nobler traits of human nature?

MEDITATION 6

- How might your sexual relationship inspire you to be a better person?

- How can knowing that the intimacy of sexual relations within marriage is right and divinely approved be a blessing for your marriage?

- Describe what a love-inspired companionship looks like to you. What is one thing you can do to move closer to that ideal?

NOTES

MEDITATION 6

Unload the Baggage

Boyd K. Packer

All of us carry excess baggage around from time to time, but the wisest ones among us don't carry it for very long. They get rid of it.

Some of it you have to get rid of without really solving the problem. Some things that ought to be put in order are not put in order because you can't control them.

Often, however, the things we carry are petty, even stupid. If you are still upset after all these years because Aunt Clara didn't come to your wedding reception, why don't you grow up? Forget it.

If you brood constantly over some past mistake, settle it—look ahead.

If the bishop didn't call you right—or release you right—forget it.

If you resent someone for something he has done—or failed to do—forget it. ("The Balm of Gilead," *Ensign*, Nov. 1977)

Jeffrey R. Holland

Surely each of us could cite an endless array of old scars and sorrows and painful memories that this very moment still corrode the peace in someone's heart or family or neighborhood. Whether we have caused that pain or been the recipient of the pain, those wounds need to be healed so that life can be as rewarding as God intended it to be. Like the food in your refrigerator that your grandchildren carefully check in your behalf, those old grievances have long since exceeded their expiration date. Please don't give precious space in your soul to them any longer. ("The Ministry of Reconciliation," *Ensign*, Nov. 2018)

Neil L. Andersen

Never give up—however deep the wounds of your soul, whatever their source, wherever or whenever they happen, and however short or long they persist, you are not meant to perish spiritually. [. . .]

MEDITATION 7

[. . .] Our Lord and Savior, Jesus Christ, through the incalculable gift of His Atonement, not only saves us from death and offers us, through repentance, forgiveness for our sins, but He also stands ready to save us from the sorrows and pains of our wounded souls.

The Savior is our Good Samaritan, sent "to heal the brokenhearted." [. . .] With compassion, He places His healing balm on our wounds and binds them up. He carries us. He cares for us. He bids us, "Come unto me . . . and I shall heal (you)." ("Wounded," *Ensign*, Nov. 2018)

PONDER AND DISCUSS:

— How can emotional baggage from the past keep you from connecting with your spouse in the present?

— Have either you or your spouse ever experienced any emotional or physical trauma or abuse that makes connection uncomfortable?

— Are there circumstances related to your mental health, lifestyle, and/or career that might be keeping you from connecting better with your spouse?

— How can the Savior help you unload your baggage?

— What professional, religious, and/or extended family resources can you reach out to as an individual and as a couple to help with this unloading and healing process?

— What is one thing, belief, or experience you can let go of that will allow you to more fully connect with your spouse? With others?

MEDITATION 7

Sexuality Comes from God

"The Family: A Proclamation to the World"
> WE DECLARE the means by which mortal life is created to be divinely appointed.

PONDER AND DISCUSS:

- How do you feel about sexuality knowing that it is divinely appointed?

- If God is the author of sexuality, and therefore knows the most about it, have you ever considered going to Him to find answers?

- What question would you ask Him first?

MEDITATION 8

Sex Within Marriage Is Sanctifying

Joseph F. Smith

Sexual union is lawful in wedlock, and, if participated in with right intent is honorable and sanctifying. (*Teachings of Presidents of the Church: Joseph F. Smith* [Salt Lake City: The Church of Jesus Christ of Latter-day Saints, 1998], 158)

Wendy Watson Nelson

Marital intimacy endorsed by the Spirit is blessed by the Lord and is sanctifying. ("Love and Marriage" [worldwide devotional for young adults, Jan. 8, 2017], churchofjesuschrist.org/broadcasts)

PONDER AND DISCUSS:

— When it comes to sexual union, what might constitute the right intent?

— How might you honor your sexual union?

— How would you define marital intimacy?

— What does marital intimacy endorsed by the Spirit look like to you? What does it feel like to you?

— What is one thing you can do to make your married sexual relationship more sanctifying?

MEDITATION 9

Sex Within Marriage Is Encouraged

Spencer W. Kimball

Husband and wife . . . are authorized, in fact they are commanded, to have proper sex when they are properly married for time and eternity. (*The Teachings of Spencer W. Kimball*, ed. Edward L. Kimball [Salt Lake City: Bookcraft, Inc., 1982], 312)

"The Family: A Proclamation to the World"

HUSBAND AND WIFE have a solemn responsibility to love and care for each other.

Wendy Watson Nelson

As an important part of the expression of their love, the Lord wants a husband and wife to partake of the wonders and joys of marital intimacy. Marital intimacy is ordained by God. It is commanded and commended by Him because it draws a husband and wife closer together and closer to the Lord! ("Love and Marriage" [worldwide devotional for young adults, Jan. 8, 2017], churchofjesuschrist.org/broadcasts)

PONDER AND DISCUSS:

— How would you define proper sex in your marriage? How has your definition of proper sex evolved over the course of your marriage?

— Why do you think married couples are commanded to engage with each other sexually?

MEDITATION 10

- What are some of the blessings you and your spouse receive by keeping this commandment?

- Why might it be important for husbands and wives to engage sexually on a regular basis? How would you define what that regular basis is for your marriage?

- What is one thing you can do to better fulfill your solemn responsibility to love and care for your spouse?

NOTES

MEDITATION 10

The Laws and Blessings of Marriage and Sexuality

Doctrine and Covenants 130:20–21

> There is a law, irrevocably decreed in heaven before the foundations of this world, upon which all blessings are predicated—
>
> And when we obtain any blessing from God, it is by obedience to that law upon which it is predicated.

PONDER AND DISCUSS:

- What are the blessings of a good marriage?
- What might some of the laws be upon which good marriages are predicated?
- What are you and your spouse doing to follow those laws in order to obtain the blessings of a good marriage? What is one thing you can do to improve?
- What are the blessings of good sexuality?
- What might some of the laws be upon which good sexuality is predicated?
- What are you and your spouse doing to follow those laws in order to obtain the blessings of good sexuality within your marriage? What is one thing you can do to improve?

MEDITATION 11

The Law of the Harvest

Galatians 6:7

> For whatsoever a man soweth, that shall he also reap.

Doctrine and Covenants 6:33

> Fear not to do good, my sons, for whatsoever ye sow, that shall ye also reap; therefore, if ye sow good ye shall also reap good for your reward.

Lawrence M. Barry

> Like the flowers, fruits, and vegetables we grow in our gardens, our marriages reflect the nature of the seeds we have planted. If we have tried throughout our married life to plant seeds of love and harmony, then we are more likely to enjoy a rich harvest. Of course, the opposite can also be true. At any given moment, we are the sum of all our sowings. ("Marriage and the Law of the Harvest," *Ensign*, Feb. 1986)

PONDER AND DISCUSS:

- How might the law of the harvest apply to your marriage? Your sexual relationship?
- What are some of the seeds that husbands and wives might sow in order to reap a happy marriage relationship?
- What are some of the seeds that husbands and wives might sow in order to reap a rich and healthy sexual relationship?
- What is one thing you can to do to keep from sowing the wrong seeds?
- What is one thing you can do to sow a good seed this week?

MEDITATION 12

Marital Priorities

D. Todd Christofferson

[Lucifer] fights to discourage marriage and the formation of families, and where marriages and families are formed, he does what he can to disrupt them. He attacks everything that is sacred about human sexuality, tearing it from the context of marriage with a seemingly infinite array of immoral thoughts and acts. He seeks to convince men and women that marriage and family priorities can be ignored or abandoned, or at least made subservient to careers, other achievements, and the quest for self-fulfillment and individual autonomy. ("Why Marriage, Why Family," *Ensign*, May 2015)

Russell M. Nelson

As I meet with priesthood leaders, I often ask about the priorities of their various responsibilities. Usually they mention their important Church duties to which they have been called. Too few remember their responsibilities at home. Yet priesthood offices, keys, callings, and quorums are meant to exalt families. Priesthood authority has been restored so that families can be sealed eternally. So brethren, your foremost priesthood duty is to nurture your marriage—to care for, respect, honor, and love your wife. ("Nurturing Marriage," *Ensign*, May 2006)

If marriage is a prime relationship in life, it deserves prime time! ("Listen to Learn," *Ensign*, May 1991)

MEDITATION 13

PONDER AND DISCUSS:

- What can you do to protect your marriage from being ignored or made subservient to careers and other achievements?

- Have you considered asking your spouse what you can do to make him/her feel like your highest priority?

- How can you protect your marriage from Satan's attacks?

- What is one thing your spouse can do to care for, respect, honor, and love you better?

- How can you regularly schedule prime time with your spouse for dating? For intimacy?

MEDITATION 13

Our Bodies Are Sacred

1 Corinthians 3:16–17

> Know ye not that ye are the temple of God, and that the Spirit of God dwelleth in you?
>
> If any man defile the temple of God, him shall God destroy; for the temple of God is holy, which temple ye are.

Jeffrey R. Holland

> A body is *the* great prize of mortal life. ("Of Souls, Symbols, and Sacraments" [Brigham Young University devotional, Jan. 12, 1988], 4, speeches.byu.edu)

Joseph Smith

> The great principle of happiness consists in having a body. The devil has no body, and herein is his punishment. (*Teachings of Presidents of the Church: Joseph Smith* [Salt Lake City: The Church of Jesus Christ of Latter-day Saints, 2007], 211)

David A. Bednar

> Our physical bodies make possible a breadth, a depth, and an intensity of experience that simply could not be obtained in our premortal estate. ("Things as They Really Are," *Ensign*, June 2010)

PONDER AND DISCUSS:

— How is your body like a temple?

— What is one thing you can do to show more respect for your own body?

— What is one thing you can do to show more respect for your spouse's body?

MEDITATION 14

- How is caring for your own body a gift to your spouse?
- When have you felt the blessing of a breadth, depth, and intensity of experience with your physical body?

NOTES _____

_____

_____

_____

_____

_____

_____

_____

_____

_____

MEDITATION 14

Our Bodies Are Beautiful

Genesis 1:27

> So God created man in his own image, in the image of God created he him; male and female created he them.

Russell M. Nelson

> Ponder the magnificence of what you see when you look in the mirror. Ignore the freckles, the unruly hair, or the blemishes, and look beyond to see the real you—a child of God, created by Him in His image. When you sing "I Am a Child of God," think of His gift to you of your own physical body. The many amazing attributes of your body attest to your own "divine nature." [. . .]
>
> [. . .] Anyone who studies the workings of the human body has surely "seen God moving in his majesty and power." ("Your Body: A Magnificent Gift to Cherish," *New Era*, Aug. 2019)

PONDER AND DISCUSS:

— If God is perfect, and has all power and all knowledge, what might that say about the body He has? What might that say about the bodies He created for us?

— How do you feel about your body?

— What does your spouse do that helps you feel beautiful?

— How might studying the workings of the human body, including sexual anatomy, help you to be a better lover?

— What is one thing you can do to quiet any internal or external voices that shame your body?

MEDITATION 15

Bridle All Your Passions

Alma 38:12

Use boldness, but not overbearance; and also see that ye bridle all your passions, that ye may be filled with love.

David A. Bednar

Love increases through righteous restraint and decreases through impulsive indulgence. ("We Believe in Being Chaste," *Ensign*, May 2013)

PONDER AND DISCUSS:

- What does it mean to you to bridle your passions?
- Why might God have implanted passions within you that need bridling?
- What is the difference between bridling your passions and rejecting or stifling your passions?
- As part of bridling your passions, how do you control your thoughts, your words, and your actions?
- What does the bridling of passions look like within your marriage relationship?
- How do you ensure your passions are in harmony with the passions, thoughts, and feelings of your spouse?
- What can you do to keep your sexual passions focused on your spouse?
- How does bridling your passions fill you with love?

MEDITATION 16

Meaningful Touch

Luke 8:43–48

And a woman having an issue of blood twelve years, which had spent all her living upon physicians, neither could be healed of any,

Came behind him, and touched the border of his garment: and immediately her issue of blood stanched.

And Jesus said, Who touched me? When all denied, Peter and they that were with him said, Master, the multitude throng thee and press thee, and sayest thou, Who touched me?

And Jesus said, Somebody hath touched me: for I perceive that virtue is gone out of me.

And when the woman saw that she was not hid, she came trembling, and falling down before him, she declared unto him before all the people for what cause she had touched him, and how she was healed immediately.

And he said unto her, Daughter, be of good comfort: thy faith hath made thee whole; go in peace.

PONDER AND DISCUSS:

— Christ had been thronged and pressed by an entire multitude, but it was the touch of the woman with the issue of blood that caught his attention. What was different?

— How can you be better at sharing touch with your spouse that is mindful, intentional, and filled with love?

— How can physical touch within marriage be healing?

— How is touch often a superior communication method compared to words?

MEDITATION 17

- How is faith involved with the touch you give and receive in your marriage?
- What is one thing your spouse can do to make your physical connections more meaningful for you?

NOTES _____

_____

_____

_____

_____

_____

_____

_____

_____

_____

MEDITATION 17

A Symbol of Total Union

Jeffrey R. Holland

May I suggest that human intimacy, that sacred, physical union ordained of God for a married couple, deals with a *symbol* that demands special sanctity. Such an act of love between a man and a woman is—or certainly was ordained to be—a symbol of total union: union of their hearts, their hopes, their lives, their love, their family, their future, their everything. It is a symbol that we try to suggest in the temple with a word like *seal*. [. . .]

As delicate as it is to mention [. . .], I nevertheless trust your maturity to understand that physiologically we are created as men and women to fit together in such a union. In this ultimate physical expression of one man and one woman they are as nearly and as literally "one" as two separate physical bodies can ever be. It is in that act of ultimate physical intimacy we most nearly fulfill the commandment of the Lord given to Adam and Eve, living symbols for all married couples, when he invited them to cleave unto one another only, and thus become "one flesh." [. . .]

[. . .] Sexual intimacy is not only a symbolic union between a man and a woman—the uniting of their very souls—but it is also symbolic of a union between mortals and deity, between otherwise ordinary and fallible humans uniting for a rare and special moment with God himself and all the powers by which he gives life in this wide universe of ours. ("Of Souls, Symbols, and Sacraments" [Brigham Young University devotional, Jan. 12, 1988], 5, speeches.byu.edu)

MEDITATION 18

Wendy Watson Nelson

True marital intimacy involves the whole soul of each spouse. It is the uniting of the body *and* the spirit of the husband with the body *and* the spirit of his wife.

That soulful union represents just how united a husband and wife are in *all* areas of their lives. ("Love and Marriage" [worldwide devotional for young adults, Jan. 8, 2017], churchofjesuschrist.org/broadcasts)

PONDER AND DISCUSS:

- How might male and female bodies be two halves of a complete whole?
- How has sexual intimacy united you with your spouse?
- What is one thing you can do to unite in deeper union with your spouse?
- How might sexual intimacy deepen your union with God?

MEDITATION 18

The Purposes of Sexuality

Ezra Taft Benson

Sex was created and established by our Heavenly Father for sacred, holy, and high purposes. (*The Teachings of Ezra Taft Benson* [Salt Lake City: Bookcraft, Inc., 1988], 409)

PONDER AND DISCUSS:

- What might some of the sacred, holy, and high purposes of sex be?
- How can you and your spouse effectively discover the various purposes of sex?
- How do different sexual rituals within your marriage meet those purposes?
- Is there anything you can eliminate that might be inhibiting the sacred, holy, and high purposes of sex within your marriage?
- What is one thing you can do to give your sexual interactions a higher purpose?

MEDITATION 19

Husbands and Wives Are Better Together

Genesis 2:18

And the Lord God said, It is not good that the man should be alone; I will make him an help meet for him.

David A. Bednar

The natures of male and female spirits complete and perfect each other, and therefore men and women are intended to progress together toward exaltation. ("Marriage Is Essential to His Eternal Plan," *Liahona*, June 2006)

PONDER AND DISCUSS:

- How are men and women bettered by being together?
- What protections might we enjoy when we are with our spouse?
- How has your marriage helped you to progress temporally? Spiritually?
- How can spouses best help each other reach their potential?

MEDITATION 20

Celestial Marriage Is Essential to Exaltation

Doctrine and Covenants 131:1–4

> In the celestial glory there are three heavens or degrees;
>
> And in order to obtain the highest, a man must enter into this order of the priesthood [meaning the new and everlasting covenant of marriage];
>
> And if he does not, he cannot obtain it.
>
> He may enter into the other, but that is the end of his kingdom; he cannot have an increase.

1 Corinthians 11:11

> Nevertheless neither is the man without the woman, neither the woman without the man, in the Lord.

Joseph F. Smith

> No man can be saved and exalted in the kingdom of God without the woman, and no woman can reach the perfection and exaltation in the kingdom of God alone. [. . .] [God] made man in his own image and likeness, male and female, and in their creation it was designed that they should be united together in sacred bonds of marriage, and one is not perfect without the other. (*Gospel Doctrine* [Salt Lake City: Deseret Book Company, 1939], 272)

PONDER AND DISCUSS:

- How are men and women imperfect without each other?
- Why do you think celestial marriage is a requirement for exaltation?

MEDITATION 21

- What might your relationship with your spouse in the eternities look like if you were not sealed?

- What are you doing to ensure that your marriage models the covenants and promises you made as part of the sealing ceremony? What is one thing you can do better?

- How might performing temple sealings with your spouse strengthen your marriage?

NOTES _____

_____

_____

_____

_____

_____

_____

_____

_____

MEDITATION 21

Love Each Other

Ephesians 5:25–29

Husbands, love your wives, even as Christ also loved the church, and gave himself for it;

That he might sanctify and cleanse it with the washing of water by the word,

That he might present it to himself a glorious church, not having spot, or wrinkle, or any such thing; but that it should be holy and without blemish.

So ought men to love their wives as their own bodies. He that loveth his wife loveth himself.

For no man ever yet hated his own flesh; but nourisheth and cherisheth it, even as the Lord the church.

Gordon B. Hinckley

Brethren, treat your wives with love and respect and kindness. And, wives, you treat your husbands with love and respect and kindness. (*Teachings of Gordon B. Hinckley* [Salt Lake City: Deseret Book Company, 1997], 209)

PONDER AND DISCUSS:

— What are some ways that your spouse follows the example of Christ in his/her love for you?

— How can you love your spouse as your own body?

— What are some things that your spouse does that help you feel loved and cherished?

MEDITATION 22

- How would you define respect? What are some things that your spouse does that help you feel respected?

- What is one thing you can do to nourish and cherish your marriage relationship?

NOTES _____

_____
_____
_____
_____
_____
_____
_____
_____
_____
_____

MEDITATION 22

Giving and Receiving

2 Corinthians 9:7

For God loveth a cheerful giver.

Doctrine and Covenants 50:22

Wherefore, he that preacheth and he that receiveth, understand one another, and both are edified and rejoice together.

Mark 14:3–6

And being in Bethany in the house of Simon the leper, as he sat at meat, there came a woman having an alabaster box of ointment of spikenard very precious; and she brake the box, and poured it on his head.

And there were some that had indignation within themselves, and said, Why was this waste of the ointment made?

For it might have been sold for more than three hundred pence, and have been given to the poor. And they murmured against her.

And Jesus said, Let her alone; why trouble ye her? she hath wrought a good work on me.

PONDER AND DISCUSS:

— What roles do giving and receiving play in your marriage?

— Like Christ's example, how can you be a better receiver?

— When it comes to sexual giving, how can you be a cheerful giver?

MEDITATION 23

- How can a loving sexual exchange be simultaneously pleasurable for both the giver and the receiver so that both are edified together?

- What gifts do you enjoy receiving from your spouse?

- What is one thing you can do to be a better giver?

NOTES

MEDITATION 23

Enjoy Your Love Together

Proverbs 5:18–19

Let thy fountain be blessed: and rejoice with the wife of thy youth.

Let her be as the loving hind and pleasant roe; let her breasts satisfy thee at all times; and be thou ravished always with her love.

Russell M. Nelson

Celebrate and commemorate each day together as a treasured gift from heaven. ("Nurturing Marriage," *Ensign*, May 2006)

PONDER AND DISCUSS:

— What might you and your spouse do to keep your marriage vibrant?

— What can you do to ensure that your spouse is the singular source of your sexual satisfaction?

— How can you and your spouse celebrate and commemorate each day together?

— What is one thing you can do to rejoice with your spouse and be ravished with his/her love?

MEDITATION 24

Higher Thoughts

Isaiah 55:8–9

> For my thoughts are not your thoughts, neither are your ways my ways, saith the Lord.
>
> For as the heavens are higher than the earth, so are my ways higher than your ways, and my thoughts than your thoughts.

PONDER AND DISCUSS:

- How are God's views about marriage and sexuality different than the world's views?

- How can you best teach God's views of marriage and sexuality to your children?

- How can you encourage your children to seek answers to questions about marriage and sexual intimacy from trustworthy sources?

- How might you elevate your views on marriage and sexuality?

- How might elevating your thoughts and ways in regard to marriage and sexuality enrich your relationship?

MEDITATION 25

Worldly Sex Versus Marital Intimacy

Wendy Watson Nelson

While worldly sex is lustful and kills love, marital intimacy generates more love.

Worldly sex degrades men and women and their bodies, while marital intimacy honors men and women and celebrates the body as one of the great prizes of mortal life.

With worldly sex, individuals can feel used, abused, and ultimately more lonely. With marital intimacy, spouses feel more united and loved, more nurtured and understood.

Worldly sex ravages and eventually ruins relationships. Marital intimacy strengthens marriages. It supports, heals, and hallows the lives of spouses and their marriage.

Worldly sex has been likened to the toot of a flute, while marital intimacy has been likened to the grandeur of an entire orchestra.

Worldly sex becomes a total obsession because it never fulfills its promises. God-ordained marital intimacy is glorious and will continue eternally for covenant-keeping husbands and wives. ("Love and Marriage" [worldwide devotional for young adults, Jan. 8, 2017], churchofjesuschrist.org/broadcasts)

PONDER AND DISCUSS:

- How do you view the difference between worldly sex and marital intimacy?

- What are some ways you can generate more love? Honor each other better? Celebrate the prize of your bodies?

MEDITATION 26

- What can you do to support, heal, and hallow the life of your spouse?
- What can you do to help each other keep your covenants?
- What is one thing you can do to move further away from worldly sex and closer to marital intimacy?

NOTES _____

_____

_____

_____

_____

_____

_____

_____

_____

_____

MEDITATION 26

Courteous Communication

Ephesians 4:29–31

Let no corrupt communication proceed out of your mouth, but that which is good to the use of edifying, that it may minister grace unto the hearers.

And grieve not the holy Spirit of God, whereby ye are sealed unto the day of redemption.

Let all bitterness, and wrath, and anger, and clamour, and evil speaking, be put away from you, with all malice.

Russell M. Nelson

Good communication includes taking time to plan together. Couples need private time to observe, to talk, and really listen to each other. They need to cooperate—helping each other as equal partners. They need to nurture their spiritual as well as physical intimacy. They should strive to elevate and motivate each other. Marital unity is sustained when goals are mutually understood. Good communication is also enhanced by prayer. To pray with specific mention of a spouse's good deed (or need) nurtures a marriage. ("Nurturing Marriage," *Ensign*, May 2006)

PONDER AND DISCUSS:

— Think of a time you felt edified and uplifted by something your spouse said or did for you. How can you do that for your spouse?

— How can you eliminate any communication (verbal or nonverbal) that corrupts your relationship?

— How often do you praise your spouse for his/her ideas and ways of doing things?

MEDITATION 27

- Do you schedule enough private time to observe, talk, plan, and really listen to each other?

- How do you gain mutual understanding of your individual goals? Your couple goals?

- How has prayer enhanced your communication and nurtured your marriage?

- What are you doing in your marriage to nurture your spiritual intimacy?

- What are you doing in your marriage to nurture your physical intimacy?

- What is one thing you can do to communicate in a more edifying and uplifting way?

MEDITATION 27

Seek First to Understand

Ether 1:34–37

> And the brother of Jared being a large and mighty man, and a man highly favored of the Lord, Jared, his brother, said unto him: Cry unto the Lord, that he will not confound us that we may not understand our words.
>
> And it came to pass that the brother of Jared did cry unto the Lord, and the Lord had compassion upon Jared; therefore he did not confound the language of Jared; and Jared and his brother were not confounded.
>
> Then Jared said unto his brother: Cry again unto the Lord, and it may be that he will turn away his anger from them who are our friends, that he confound not their language.
>
> And it came to pass that the brother of Jared did cry unto the Lord, and the Lord had compassion upon their friends and their families also, that they were not confounded.

PONDER AND DISCUSS:

— Why is it sometimes easy for married partners to feel confounded in their communication?

— Which discussion topics often confound you and your spouse?

— Why might it be difficult for spouses to converse about their sexuality?

— Have you thought to cry unto the Lord as the brother of Jared did, that you may not be confounded as you communicate with your spouse?

MEDITATION 28

- What is one thing you can do to make it easier for your spouse to communicate with you?
- What is one thing you can do to communicate more openly and honestly with your spouse?

NOTES _____

_____

_____

_____

_____

_____

_____

_____

_____

_____

MEDITATION 28

Mutual Acceptability

David A. Bednar

There are also bounds for the appropriate expression of love between a husband and a wife. Dignity, purity, and mutual acceptability ought to characterize our most intimate relationships. ("Moral Purity" [Brigham Young University–Idaho devotional, Jan. 7, 2003], byui.edu)

PONDER AND DISCUSS:

- How would you define dignity in regard to your intimate relationship? What does purity mean to you in your intimate relationship?

- How can you ensure that you and your spouse feel mutual acceptability in your intimate relationship?

- What can you do to better understand each other when your perceptions of acceptability differ?

- What is one thing you can do to express your love with more dignity and purity?

MEDITATION 29

A Part of Life with No Equal

Boyd K. Packer

[Procreative power] combines the most exquisite and exalted physical, emotional, and spiritual feelings associated with the word *love*. That part of life has no equal, no counterpart, in all human experience. It will, when covenants are made and kept, last eternally. ("The Plan of Happiness," *Ensign*, May 2015)

PONDER AND DISCUSS:

- How is our sexuality a combination of the physical, the emotional, and the spiritual?

- What can you do to ensure that your sexual interactions with your spouse remain exquisite and exalted?

- What can you do to ensure this intimacy lasts eternally?

MEDITATION 30

Be Fully Present

Jeffrey R. Holland

Short of being in the very presence of God, literally, you will never be more proximate to divinity than you are in the presence of your spouse [. . .] They deserve divine attention. (Tad Walch, "Elder Holland Answers Questions from Young, Married Latter-day Saints in Anglican Oxford Chapel," *Church News*, Nov. 28, 2018)

1 Samuel 3:4

That the Lord called Samuel: and he answered, Here am I.

Genesis 22:11

And the angel of the Lord called unto him out of heaven, and said, Abraham, Abraham: and he said, Here am I.

Acts 9:10

And there was a certain disciple at Damascus, named Ananias; and to him said the Lord in a vision, Ananias. And he said, Behold, I am here, Lord.

PONDER AND DISCUSS:

— What are some ways you might give your spouse divine attention?

— How can you be "here" (fully present) with your spouse when conversing together?

— What can you do to minimize distractions from electronic devices while interacting with each other?

MEDITATION 31

- How can you be fully present and mentally remain in the moment during sexual intimacy?

- What is one thing you can do to facilitate or encourage more meaningful interaction with your spouse?

NOTES _____

_____

_____

_____

_____

_____

_____

_____

_____

_____

_____

MEDITATION 31

The Choice Is Yours

Helaman 14:30

And now remember, remember, my brethren, that whosoever perisheth, perisheth unto himself; and whosoever doeth iniquity, doeth it unto himself; for behold, ye are free; ye are permitted to act for yourselves; for behold, God hath given unto you a knowledge and he hath made you free.

Spencer W. Kimball

Don't just pray to marry the one you love. *Instead, pray to love the one you marry.* (Quoted in Joe J. Christensen, "Marriage and the Great Plan of Happiness," *Ensign*, May 1995)

Dieter F. Uchtdorf

In God's plan of happiness, we are not so much looking for someone perfect but for a person with whom, throughout a lifetime, we can join efforts to create a loving, lasting, and more perfect relationship. That is the goal. ("In Praise of Those Who Save," *Ensign*, May 2016)

Marion D. Hanks

Such a marriage never *just happens*. [A strong union] is *brought about* not simply by ceremony or circumstance or chance, but by two mature, loving adults who are able and willing to learn the principles upon which a vital and durable marriage may be fashioned and who, day by day, year by year, work on that process. ("Eternal Marriage," *Ensign*, Nov. 1984)

Thomas S. Monson

Choose your love; love your choice. ("Hallmarks of a Happy Home," *Ensign*, Nov. 1988)

MEDITATION 32

PONDER AND DISCUSS:

- How is love a choice?
- How can you use your agency to love your spouse more fully?
- What might happen if you choose to make a healthy intimate relationship a priority in your marriage?
- When was the last time you made an active effort to pursue your spouse?
- How can prayer help you love the one you've married?
- What is one thing you can do to join efforts to create a loving, lasting, and more perfect relationship?

MEDITATION 32

Be Humble and Acknowledge Your Faults

Doctrine and Covenants 112:10

Be thou humble; and the Lord thy God shall lead thee by the hand, and give thee answer to thy prayers.

Dieter F. Uchtdorf

Sincerely apologizing to your children, your wife, your family, or your friends is not a sign of weakness but of strength. Is being right more important than fostering an environment of nurturing, healing, and love?

Build bridges; don't destroy them.

Even when you are not at fault—perhaps especially when you are not at fault—let love conquer pride. ("In Praise of Those Who Save," *Ensign*, May 2016)

Joe J. Christensen

To develop a solid marriage, we must be able to admit we are sorry for mistakes we make. [. . .] When conflicts in marriage arise, we should be swift to apologize and ask for forgiveness, even though we may not be totally at fault. True love is developed by those who are willing to readily admit personal mistakes and offenses. (*One Step at a Time: Building a Better Marriage, Family, and You* [Salt Lake City: Deseret Book Company, 1996], 39)

PONDER AND DISCUSS:

— In your marriage relationship, what does humility look like to you?

— How can we get over the reluctance to admit our fault when we are wrong?

MEDITATION 33

- What elements do you feel constitute a sincere apology?
- What is one thing you can do to humbly let God lead you to a better marriage relationship?
- What is one thing you can do to let love conquer pride?

NOTES

MEDITATION 33

Frequent Forgiveness

Ephesians 4:32

> And be ye kind one to another, tenderhearted, forgiving one another, even as God for Christ's sake hath forgiven you.

Doctrine and Covenants 64:9

> Wherefore, I say unto you, that ye ought to forgive one another; for he that forgiveth not his brother his trespasses standeth condemned before the Lord; for there remaineth in him the greater sin.

PONDER AND DISCUSS:

- What does being tenderhearted look like to you?
- How has the principle of forgiveness blessed you in your marriage?
- What might happen to your marriage if you can't forgive your spouse for his/her imperfections and mistakes?
- What are some things you can do if you want to forgive but you're finding it hard to do so?
- What is one thing you would like to be forgiven for by your spouse?
- What is one thing that you'd like your spouse to do today to show kindness to you?

MEDITATION 34

Sincere Devotion

Ruth 1:16

> And Ruth said, Entreat me not to leave thee, or to return from following after thee: for whither thou goest, I will go; and where thou lodgest, I will lodge: thy people shall be my people, and thy God my God.

PONDER AND DISCUSS:

- What are the rewards of loyalty between husband and wife?
- What can you and your spouse do to maintain closeness when you are geographically separated for extended periods?
- In regard to your marriage, what can you do to ensure emotional fidelity as well as physical fidelity?
- How has your relationship grown by lodging together and sharing the same bed?
- How can you show respect for your spouse by making his/her people your people and his/her family your family?
- What is one thing you can do to worship God and grow spiritually together?
- Following the example of Ruth, what is one thing you can do to demonstrate sincere devotion to your spouse?

MEDITATION 35

Marriage and Sexuality as Divine Gifts

Matthew 7:9–11

> Or what man is there of you, whom if his son ask bread, will he give him a stone? Or if he ask a fish, will he give him a serpent?
>
> If ye then, being evil, know how to give good gifts unto your children, how much more shall your Father which is in heaven give good things to them that ask him?

Doctrine and Covenants 88:33

> For what doth it profit a man if a gift is bestowed upon him, and he receive not the gift? Behold, he rejoices not in that which is given unto him, neither rejoices in him who is the giver of the gift.

L. Whitney Clayton

> Marriage is a gift from God to us; the quality of our marriages is a gift from us to Him. ("Marriage: Watch and Learn," *Ensign*, May 2013)

PONDER AND DISCUSS:

— How is marriage a gift from God to us? How can you show gratitude for this gift?

— How might sexuality be a gift from God? How might God feel if His gift to you is unopened, underutilized, unappreciated, or unenjoyed?

— How can you receive God's gifts of marriage and sexuality more fully? How can you better share these gifts with your spouse?

MEDITATION 36

- If God is the giver of these gifts, how might He help you receive them and enjoy them more fully?
- What is one thing you can do to improve the quality of your marriage as a gift to God?

NOTES _____

_____

_____

_____

_____

_____

_____

_____

_____

_____

MEDITATION 36

The Significance of Biblical Terms

Genesis 4:1

And Adam knew Eve his wife; and she conceived.

David J. Whittaker

The Hebrew verb *yada* (or *da'ath*) is usually translated "to know" or "to be acquainted with." But the covenant context adds both a mental and an emotional act. In Genesis 4:1, "Adam *yada* Eve" (King James: "Adam knew Eve his wife"); that is, in their covenant relationship they had mutual obligations and mutual concerns. Adam acted out of concern, inner engagement, dedication, and affection for Eve. The relationship summed up as *yada* was more than just physical. ("A Covenant People: Old Testament Light on Modern Covenants," *Ensign*, Aug. 1980)

Old Testament Student Manual 1 Kings–Malachi, 3rd Ed.

The Hebrew word *yada*, which is translated *knew*, connotes a very personal, intimate relationship. ("As Ye Sow, So Shall Ye Reap" [Salt Lake City: The Church of Jesus Christ of Latter-day Saints, 2003], 235)

Genesis 26:8

Abimelech king of the Philistines looked out at a window, and saw, and, behold, Isaac was sporting with Rebekah his wife.

MEDITATION 37

PONDER AND DISCUSS:

- Why might the term "knew" be used to describe sexual activity?

- How is intimacy about truly knowing? How is intimacy about knowing truth?

- What can you do to know your spouse better? What can your spouse do to know you better?

- What is it about sexual intimacy that helps us to really know, understand, and comprehend each other better?

- Why might the term "sporting" be used to describe sexual activity? How can you and your spouse be more playful in the bedroom?

- Why is it important to spend time together as husband and wife just having fun?

- What is one thing you and your spouse can do to have fun and laugh together this week?

MEDITATION 37

Keep Christ as Your Center

Doctrine and Covenants 6:36

Look unto me in every thought; doubt not, fear not.

Russell M. Nelson

Marriage is sanctified when it is cherished and honored in holiness. That union is not merely between husband and wife; it embraces a partnership with God. ("Nurturing Marriage," *Ensign*, May 2006)

David A. Bednar

The Lord Jesus Christ is the focal point in a covenant marriage relationship. Please notice how the Savior is positioned at the apex of this triangle, with a woman at the base of one corner and a man at the base of the other corner. Now consider what happens in the relationship between the man and the woman as they individually and steadily "come unto Christ" and strive to be "perfected in Him" (Moroni 10:32). Because of and through the Redeemer, the man and the woman come closer together. ("Marriage is Essential to His Eternal Plan," *Liahona*, June 2006)

PONDER AND DISCUSS:

— How might looking unto Christ in every thought help you in your marriage?

— How might looking unto Christ ease your doubts and calm your fears?

MEDITATION 38

- How does Elder Bednar's triangle example help you understand your marriage partnership with your spouse and God?
- What is one thing you can do to steadily come closer to your spouse?
- What is one thing you can do together to steadily come closer to Christ?

NOTES

MEDITATION 38

The Source of Lasting Fulfillment

John 4:7, 9–18

There cometh a woman of Samaria to draw water: Jesus saith unto her, Give me to drink. [. . .]

Then saith the woman of Samaria unto him, How is it that thou, being a Jew, askest drink of me, which am a woman of Samaria? for the Jews have no dealings with the Samaritans.

Jesus answered and said unto her, If thou knewest the gift of God, and who it is that saith to thee, Give me to drink; thou wouldest have asked of him, and he would have given thee living water.

The woman saith unto him, Sir, thou hast nothing to draw with, and the well is deep: from whence then hast thou that living water?

Art thou greater than our father Jacob, which gave us the well, and drank thereof himself, and his children, and his cattle?

Jesus answered and said unto her, Whosoever drinketh of this water shall thirst again:

But whosoever drinketh of the water that I shall give him shall never thirst; but the water that I shall give him shall be in him a well of water springing up into everlasting life.

The woman saith unto him, Sir, give me this water, that I thirst not, neither come hither to draw.

Jesus saith unto her, Go, call thy husband, and come hither.

The woman answered and said, I have no husband. Jesus said unto her, Thou hast well said, I have no husband:

For thou hast had five husbands; and he whom thou now hast is not thy husband: in that saidst thou truly.

MEDITATION 39

PONDER AND DISCUSS:

- What fulfillment might the woman at the well have been looking for in her marriage that her husbands could not provide?

- What living water and satisfaction can Christ provide that is unrealistic to expect from your spouse?

- How might the woman at the well have been under the illusion that a new marriage partner would solve her problems?

- How might prioritizing your relationship with Christ stabilize and enhance your marriage relationship? All of your other relationships?

MEDITATION 39

The Verity of the Covenant

L. Tom Perry
The entire theology of our restored gospel centers on families and on the new and everlasting covenant of marriage. ("Why Marriage and Family Matter—Everywhere in the World," *Ensign*, May 2015)

Bruce C. Hafen
Marriage is by nature a covenant, not just a private contract one may cancel at will. Jesus taught about contractual attitudes when he described the "hireling," who performs his conditional promise of care only when he receives something in return. When the hireling "seeth the wolf coming," he "leaveth the sheep, and fleeth . . . because he . . . careth not for the sheep." By contrast, the Savior said, "I am the good shepherd, . . . and I lay down my life for the sheep." Many people today marry as hirelings. And when the wolf comes, they flee. This idea is wrong. It curses the earth, turning parents' hearts away from their children and from each other. ("Covenant Marriage," *Ensign*, Nov. 1996)

Ezra Taft Benson
Marriage itself must be regarded as a sacred covenant before God. A married couple have an obligation not only to each other, but to God. He has promised blessings to those who honor that covenant. ("Fundamentals of Enduring Family Relationships," *Ensign*, Nov. 1982)

Richard G. Scott
The temple sealing has greater meaning as life unfolds. It will help you draw ever closer together and find greater joy and fulfillment in mortality. ("The Eternal Blessings of Marriage," *Ensign*, May 2011)

PONDER AND DISCUSS:

- What is the difference between a covenant and a private contract that one may cancel at will?

- Why is the word "covenant" used in conjunction with marriage? How does viewing your marriage as a covenant influence you and your relationship?

- When it comes to the marriage covenant, what are some of the promises you make to your spouse and to God?

- What are some of the blessings God promises to you as you faithfully observe the marriage covenant?

- What is one thing you can do to better fulfill your part of the marriage covenant?

MEDITATION 40

The Joy of Marital Intimacy

Russell M. Nelson

> Marriage between a man and a woman is fundamental to the Lord's doctrine and crucial to God's eternal plan. Marriage between a man and a woman is God's pattern for a fulness of life on earth and in heaven. God's marriage pattern cannot be abused, misunderstood, or misconstrued. Not if you want true joy. God's marriage pattern protects the sacred power of procreation and the joy of true marital intimacy. ("Decisions for Eternity," *Ensign*, Nov. 2013)

PONDER AND DISCUSS:

- How can your marriage help you experience a fulness of life on earth? In heaven?

- How can following God's pattern for marriage bring you true joy?

- What is one thing you can do in your marriage to experience the joy of true marital intimacy?

MEDITATION 41

Regular Rituals

2 Corinthians 13:12

Greet one another with an holy kiss.

Joseph Smith Translation, 2 Corinthians 13:12

Greet one another with an holy salutation. (In 2 Corinthians 13:12, footnote *a*)

Gary and Joy Lundberg

Taking time away from other chores to lovingly greet her husband worked. [. . .] Expressions of love like these help bring order to chaos and balance into life. ("The Marriage Balancing Act," *Ensign*, Jan. 2000)

PONDER AND DISCUSS:

- What salutation do you give to show love for your spouse when one of you is departing? When one of you arrives?

- How might a regular ritual to lovingly greet each other celebrate and strengthen your marriage?

- How can your kisses be holy?

- What is one thing you would like to do to elevate one of your regular rituals?

- What other rituals might you consider regularly incorporating in your marriage?

MEDITATION 42

The Power of Patterns

Alma 9:16
> For it is because of the traditions of their fathers that caused them to remain in their state of ignorance.

1 Nephi 18:2
> Now I, Nephi, did not work the timbers after the manner which was learned by men, neither did I build the ship after the manner of men; but I did build it after the manner which the Lord had shown unto me; wherefore, it was not after the manner of men.

PONDER AND DISCUSS:

- What traditions and patterns for healthy and happy marriages have you seen in your parents or other mentors that you have tried to implement?

- Are there any unhealthy traditions and patterns you have seen in other relationships that you have tried to avoid or eliminate?

- Do you feel your married interactions, including your sexual interactions, were taught to you after the manner of men? How might you learn to interact as a couple and build intimacy in a way that is not after the manner of men?

MEDITATION 43

- Do you feel your current sexual traditions are nourishing your marriage, strengthening your relationship, and creating the intimacy you desire? If not, how can you improve?

- As husband and wife, is your current sexual repertoire limited to a defined set of traditions or routines? Can you think of anything in your background that might have influenced this limit? What is one thing you would like to add or do differently?

NOTES

MEDITATION 43

The Power of Love

1 Corinthians 13:1–8

Though I speak with the tongues of men and of angels, and have not charity, I am become as sounding brass, or a tinkling cymbal.

And though I have the gift of prophecy, and understand all mysteries, and all knowledge; and though I have all faith, so that I could remove mountains, and have not charity, I am nothing.

And though I bestow all my goods to feed the poor, and though I give my body to be burned, and have not charity, it profiteth me nothing.

Charity suffereth long, and is kind; charity envieth not; charity vaunteth not itself, is not puffed up,

Doth not behave itself unseemly, seeketh not her own, is not easily provoked, thinketh no evil;

Rejoiceth not in iniquity, but rejoiceth in the truth;

Beareth all things, believeth all things, hopeth all things, endureth all things.

Charity never faileth.

Dieter F. Uchtdorf

The more we allow the love of God to govern our minds and emotions—the more we allow our love for our Heavenly Father to swell within our hearts—the easier it is to love others with the pure love of Christ. As we open our hearts to the glowing dawn of the love of God, the darkness and cold of animosity and envy will eventually fade. [. . .]

The pure love of Christ can remove the scales of resentment and wrath from our eyes, allowing us to see others the way our Heavenly Father sees us: as flawed and imperfect mortals who have potential and worth far beyond our capacity to imagine. ("The Merciful Obtain Mercy," *Ensign*, May 2012)

MEDITATION 44

Moroni 7:47–48

But charity is the pure love of Christ, and it endureth forever; and whoso is found possessed of it at the last day, it shall be well with him.

Wherefore, my beloved brethren, pray unto the Father with all the energy of heart, that ye may be filled with this love.

Jeffrey R. Holland

In Mormon's and Paul's final witnesses, they declare that "charity (pure love) never faileth" (Moroni 7:46, 1 Corinthians 13:8). It is there through thick and thin. It endures through sunshine and shadow, through darkest sorrow and on into the light. It *never* fails. So Christ loved us, and that is how He hoped we would love each other. In a final injunction to all his disciples for all time, He said, "A new commandment I give unto you, That ye love one another; *as I have loved you*" (John 13:34; emphasis added). Of course such Christlike staying power in romance and marriage requires more than any of us really have. It requires something more, an endowment from heaven. Remember Mormon's promise: that such love—the love we each yearn for and cling to—is "bestowed" upon "true followers of Christ." You want capability, safety, and security in dating and romance, in married life and eternity? Be a true disciple of Jesus. Be a genuine, committed, word-and-deed Latter-day Saint. Believe that your faith has *everything* to do with your romance, because it does. You separate dating from discipleship at your peril. Or, to phrase that more positively, Jesus Christ, the Light of the World, is the only lamp by which you can successfully see the path of love and happiness for you *and* for your sweetheart. How *should* I love thee? As He does, for that way "never faileth." ("How Do I Love Thee?" [Brigham Young University devotional, Feb. 15, 2000], 6, speeches.byu.edu)

MEDITATION 44

PONDER AND DISCUSS:

- How might you allow the love of God to govern your mind and emotions?

- How would loving God more fully enhance your marriage?

- How can you and your spouse better bear and endure all things together? How can you help your spouse bear and endure his/her personal stresses, trials, and infirmities?

- What does "charity never faileth" mean to you?

- When you find yourself thinking evil of your spouse, what is one thing you can do to think no evil of him/her?

- When you begin to think evil of yourself, what is one thing you can do to think no evil of and have greater charity for yourself?

- How can you overcome envy, pride, and irritability in your relationships?

- How might having an "endowment from heaven" of Christlike love enable you to love your spouse better?

- What is one thing you can do to develop greater charity for your spouse? For your family? For yourself?

MEDITATION 44

The Power of Gratitude

Russell M. Nelson

To *appreciate*—to say "I love you" and "thank you"—is not difficult. But these expressions of love and appreciation do more than acknowledge a kind thought or deed. They are signs of sweet civility. As grateful partners look for the good in each other and sincerely pay compliments to one another, wives and husbands will strive to become the persons described in those compliments. ("Nurturing Marriage," *Ensign*, May 2006)

James E. Faust

One of the evils of our time is taking for granted so many of the things we enjoy. ("Gratitude As a Saving Principle," *Ensign*, May 1990)

Doctrine and Covenants 59:7

Thou shalt thank the Lord thy God in all things.

PONDER AND DISCUSS:

— What are some specific things about your spouse that you are grateful for?

— Even with its imperfections, what can you do to show gratitude for your spouse's body? Your body?

— How can you show gratitude to God for your spouse and for your marriage?

— How might remembering to show gratitude for your spouse bless your relationship? What is one thing you can do today to show gratitude for your spouse?

MEDITATION 45

The Power of the Word

Alma 31:5

    And now, as the preaching of the word had a great tendency to lead the people to do that which was just—yea, it had had more powerful effect upon the minds of the people than the sword, or anything else, which had happened unto them—therefore Alma thought it was expedient that they should try the virtue of the word of God.

Marion G. Romney

    I feel certain that if, in our homes, parents will read from the Book of Mormon prayerfully and regularly, both by themselves and with their children, the spirit of that great book will come to permeate our homes and all who dwell therein. The spirit of reverence will increase; mutual respect and consideration for each other will grow. The spirit of contention will depart. Parents will counsel their children in greater love and wisdom. Children will be more responsive and submissive to the counsel of their parents. Righteousness will increase. Faith, hope, and charity—the pure love of Christ—will abound in our homes and lives, bringing in their wake peace, joy, and happiness. ("The Book of Mormon," *Ensign*, May 1980)

Russell M. Nelson

    Each individual who prayerfully studies the Book of Mormon can also receive a testimony of its divinity. In addition, this book can help with personal problems in a very real way. Do you want to get rid of a bad habit? Do you want to improve relationships in your family? Do you want to increase your spiritual capacity? Read the Book of Mormon! It will bring you closer to the Lord and His loving

MEDITATION 46

power. He who fed a multitude with five loaves and two fishes—He who helped the blind to see and the lame to walk—can also bless you! He has promised that those who live by the precepts of this book "shall receive a crown of eternal life." ("A Testimony of the Book of Mormon," *Ensign*, Nov. 1999)

When I think of the Book of Mormon, I think of the word *power*. The truths of the Book of Mormon have the *power* to heal, comfort, restore, succor, strengthen, console, and cheer our souls. ("The Book of Mormon: What Would Your Life Be Like without It?" *Ensign*, Nov. 2017)

PONDER AND DISCUSS:

— What are some ways personal scripture study can improve your marriage relationship? Your family relationships?

— What is one thing you can do to bring the power of the word of God into your marriage? Your family?

MEDITATION 46

The Power of Prayer and Fasting

3 Nephi 18:21

Pray in your families unto the Father, always in my name, that your wives and your children may be blessed.

Gordon B. Hinckley

I know of no single practice that will have a more salutary effect upon your lives than the practice of kneeling together as you begin and close each day. Somehow the little storms that seem to afflict every marriage are dissipated when, kneeling before the Lord, you thank him for one another, in the presence of one another, and then together invoke his blessings upon your lives, your home, your loved ones, and your dreams.

God then will be your partner, and your daily conversations with him will bring peace into your hearts and a joy into your lives that can come from no other source. Your companionship will sweeten through the years; your love will strengthen. Your appreciation for one another will grow. ("'Except the Lord Build the House . . .'" *Ensign*, June 1971)

Henry B. Eyring

I give counsel to husbands and wives. Pray for the love which allows you to see the good in your companion. Pray for the love that makes weaknesses and mistakes seem small. Pray for the love to make your companion's joy your own. Pray for the love to want to lessen the load and soften the sorrows of your companion. ("Our Perfect Example," *Ensign*, Nov. 2009)

MEDITATION 47

Carl B. Pratt

A family fast might help increase love and appreciation among family members and reduce the amount of contention in the family, or we might fast as a couple to strengthen our marriage bonds. ("The Blessings of a Proper Fast," *Ensign*, Nov. 2004)

PONDER AND DISCUSS:

- If you and your spouse aren't praying together as you begin and close each day, what is stopping you?

- When have the words of your spouse's prayer had a positive effect on you?

- What are some specific things you and your spouse can pray for together that would bless your marriage?

- Have you ever fasted for the purpose of strengthening your marriage?

- What is one thing you can do to make prayer a more integral part of your marriage?

MEDITATION 47

The Power of Faith

Alma 32:21

And now as I said concerning faith—faith is not to have a perfect knowledge of things; therefore if ye have faith ye hope for things which are not seen, which are true.

Boyd K. Packer

Some think that every marriage must expect to end in unhappiness and divorce, with the hopes and dreams predestined to end in a broken, sad wreck of things.

Some marriages do bend, and some will break, but we must not, because of this, lose faith in marriage nor become afraid of it.

Broken marriages are not typical. ("Marriage," *Ensign*, May 1981)

Jeffrey R. Holland

Let me declare unequivocally, absolutely, and adamantly that not only is there such a thing as a happy marriage, but happy marriages are the rule, not the exception.

Sister Holland and I are living proof that you can not just be happy but that you can be ecstatically happy. You can be just movingly happy in all the right ways, for all the right reasons. So I want everybody to dismiss the idea that somehow this is a mountain that can't be climbed, it's a river that can't be crossed, that there are too many difficulties to address marriage in this day or any day. That is simply not true.

You have to work at a marriage. Every good thing that I know of in this world you have to work at.

God will help you. Of all the things in this world that He will help you with, He will help you with your marriages and your families, because it matters to

Him at least as much as it matters to you. (Face to Face with Elder Holland, Sister Stephens, and Elder Hallstrom [worldwide young single adult event, March 8, 2016], churchofjesuschrist.org/broadcasts/face-to-face)

PONDER AND DISCUSS:

— How can you increase your faith in your ability to be a good husband/wife?

— What can you do to show your spouse that you have faith in your marriage?

— What role does work play in regard to having faith in your marriage?

— How can you reassure your children that a happy marriage is attainable?

— How can you help your children prepare for and sustain a happy marriage?

— What things do you hope for in your marriage that give you the faith to work at it?

MEDITATION 48

The Power of the Priesthood

Russell M. Nelson

In a coming day, *only* those men who have taken their priesthood seriously, by *diligently* seeking to be taught by the Lord Himself, will be able to bless, guide, protect, strengthen, and heal others. Only a man who has paid the price for priesthood power will be able to bring miracles to those he loves and keep his marriage and family safe, now and throughout eternity. [. . .]

In these latter days, we know there will be earthquakes in diverse places. Perhaps one of those diverse places will be in our own homes, where emotional, financial, or spiritual "earthquakes" may occur. Priesthood power can calm the seas and heal fractures in the earth. Priesthood power can also calm the minds and heal fractures in the hearts of those we love. ("The Price of Priesthood Power," *Ensign*, May 2016)

May you, your loved ones, and your posterity be blessed by your righteous pursuit of power in the priesthood. ("Personal Priesthood Responsibility," *Ensign*, Nov. 2003)

And when your wife is sealed to you, her power and potential will increase yours. ("Personal Priesthood Responsibility," *Ensign*, Nov. 2003)

Jean B. Bingham

Being endowed with *priesthood power*—God's power—means having greater power to press forward in fulfilling God's purposes. [. . .]

[. . .] How will I act differently because I have been endowed with priesthood power? What does it mean in my marriage to be endowed with priesthood power? [. . .] I have been given a gift of power—power to receive revelation, power to act.

MEDITATION 49

How do I act differently? What difference does it make for me? ("Endowed with Priesthood Power" [Brigham Young University Women's Conference address, May 2, 2019], 3, womensconference.byu.edu)

Sharon Eubank

Doctrine and Covenants 121 [. . .] is specifically for us—a divine handbook on what it means to be endowed with priesthood power. [. . .] It basically says this: it can't be used to control unrighteously, it can only be used to love. [. . .]

[. . .] This is one of the most transcendent promises in all scripture. It is about priesthood and it is for all of God's daughters and sons. ("Endowed with Priesthood Power" [Brigham Young University Women's Conference address, May 2, 2019], 11, womensconference.byu.edu)

PONDER AND DISCUSS:

- What might priesthood power have to do with keeping your marriage safe? Your family safe? How might priesthood power keep your marriage safe now? Throughout eternity?

- How might priesthood power heal fractures in your heart?

- What does it mean in your marriage for each of you to be endowed with priesthood power? How might the power of the priesthood help you to love better?

- How have you been blessed by receiving priesthood blessings from your husband? By giving priesthood blessings to your wife?

- What is one thing you and your spouse can do to increase priesthood power in your home?

MEDITATION 49

Share Feelings

Marvin J. Ashton

If we would know true love and understanding one for another, we must realize that communication is more than a sharing of words. It is the *wise* sharing of emotions, feelings, and concerns. It is the sharing of oneself totally. ("Family Communications," *Ensign*, May 1976)

Russell M. Nelson

Husbands and wives, learn to listen, and listen to learn from one another. [. . .]

Even with normal hearing, some couples seem not to listen to one another. ("Listen to Learn," *Ensign*, May 1991)

C. Richard Chidester

In intimate relationships, we share feelings we normally keep hidden—doubts and fears, joys and sorrows, hopes and dreams. Most people marry out of a hunger for intimacy, but few achieve it. In fact, I feel that a great deal of suffering and loneliness in relationships can be traced back to a lack of intimacy.

Intimacy, then, means sharing feelings. [. . .]

It's a thrilling thing when couples and families can throw off their taboos about showing emotions and can communicate about their feelings, when they listen and speak to each other with sensitivity, and when they—sometimes for the first time—experience intimacy. I'll never forget one man who came to believe that sharing his feelings was a sign of strength, not weakness, and told his wife how he'd been feeling about himself. Seeing her receive his words with gratitude and relief and understanding, he exclaimed with the light of discovery in his face, "It's a whole new world, isn't it!" ("Keeping in Touch with Feelings," *Ensign*, July 1979)

MEDITATION 50

PONDER AND DISCUSS:

- What does the wise sharing of emotions, feelings, and concerns look like to you?

- How can you more effectively share your emotions, feelings, and concerns with your spouse?

- How can you share negative or uncomfortable feelings without placing blame for those feelings on your spouse?

- What can you do to make it easier for your spouse to communicate his/her doubts and fears, joys and sorrows, hopes and dreams?

- What is one thing you can do to be a better listener so that your spouse feels more comfortable sharing his/her feelings?

- What one feeling, hope, concern, doubt, or joy would you like to share with your spouse today?

MEDITATION 50

Practice Self-Care

Brigham Young

Then let us seek to extend the present life to the uttermost, by observing every law of health, and by properly balancing labor, study, rest, and recreation, and thus prepare for a better life. (*Teachings of Presidents of the Church: Brigham Young* [Salt Lake City: The Church of Jesus Christ of Latter-day Saints, 1997], 214)

For the Strength of Youth

To care for your body, eat nutritious food, exercise regularly, and get enough sleep. Practice balance and moderation in all aspects of your physical health. Also, avoid extremes in diet that could lead to eating disorders. Do not intentionally harm your body. Avoid dangerous activities that put your body at risk of serious injury. ("Physical and Emotional Health" [booklet, Salt Lake City: The Church of Jesus Christ of Latter-day Saints, 2011], 25)

Mosiah 4:27

And see that all these things are done in wisdom and order; for it is not requisite that a man should run faster than he has strength. And again, it is expedient that he should be diligent, that thereby he might win the prize; therefore, all things must be done in order.

MEDITATION 51

PONDER AND DISCUSS:

- How can taking care of your own physical body help you be a better marriage partner?

- Do you have any health issues, diagnosed or undiagnosed, that make connecting with your spouse difficult or uncomfortable? Is there something keeping you from seeking professional help?

- What lifestyle choices can you make that would reduce stress in your life? How can doing things in wisdom and order help you to be a better marriage partner?

- What is one thing you can do to improve your care for yourself?

MEDITATION 51

Accommodate Life's Rhythms

Ecclesiastes 3:1

To every thing there is a season, and a time to every purpose under the heaven.

James E. Faust

You cannot do all these things well at the same time. You cannot eat all of the pastries in the baking shop at once. You will get a tummyache. You cannot be a 100-percent wife, a 100-percent mother, a 100-percent Church worker, a 100-percent career person, and a 100-percent public-service person at the same time. How can all of these roles be coordinated? I suggest that you can have it sequentially.

Sequentially is a big word meaning to do things one at a time at different times. ("How Near to the Angels," *Ensign*, May 1998)

Jeffrey R. Holland

As a youth in England, Samuel Plimsoll was fascinated with watching ships load and unload their cargoes. He soon observed that, regardless of the cargo space available, each ship had its maximum capacity. If a ship exceeded its limit, it would likely sink at sea. In 1868 Plimsoll entered Parliament and passed a merchant shipping act that, among other things, called for making calculations of how much a ship could carry. As a result, lines were drawn on the hull of each ship in England. As the cargo was loaded, the freighter would sink lower and lower into the water. When the water level on the side of the ship reached the Plimsoll mark, the ship was considered loaded to capacity, regardless of how much space remained. As a result, British deaths at sea were greatly reduced.

Like ships, people have differing capacities at different times and even different days in their lives. In our relationships we need to establish our own Plimsoll marks and help identify them in the lives of those we love. Together we

MEDITATION 52

need to monitor the load levels and be helpful in shedding or at least readjusting some cargo if we see our sweetheart is sinking. Then, when the ship of love is stabilized, we can evaluate long-term what has to continue, what can be put off until another time, and what can be put off permanently. Friends, sweethearts, and spouses need to be able to monitor each other's stress and recognize the different tides and seasons of life. We owe it to each other to declare some limits and then help jettison some things if emotional health and the strength of loving relationships are at risk. Remember, pure love "beareth all things, believeth all things, hopeth all things, endureth all things," and helps loved ones do the same. ("How Do I Love Thee?" [Brigham Young University devotional, Feb. 15, 2000], 5–6, speeches.byu.edu)

PONDER AND DISCUSS:

— How is the current rhythm of your life—including children, careers, callings, health, and so forth—affecting your ability to connect with your spouse?

— In relation to marital intimacy, what can you do to better adapt to fluctuating hormones and reproductive cycles?

— What strategies can you employ to maintain a healthy intimate connection during pregnancy? Postnatal periods?

— What strategies can you employ to maintain a healthy intimate connection during periods of illness or disability?

— How can you keep your intimate connection alive as you age?

— What is one thing you can do in respect to life's rhythms that will enable you to connect better with your spouse?

MEDITATION 52

Labor Together in Love

Moses 5:1

And it came to pass that after I, the Lord God, had driven them out, that Adam began to till the earth, and to have dominion over all the beasts of the field, and to eat his bread by the sweat of his brow, as I the Lord had commanded him. And Eve, also, his wife, did labor with him.

Ezra Taft Benson

Woman was given to man as an helpmeet. That complementary association is ideally portrayed in the eternal marriage of our first parents—Adam and Eve. They labored together; they had children together; they prayed together; and they taught their children the gospel together. This is the pattern God would have all righteous men and women imitate. ("The Honored Place of Woman," *Ensign*, Nov. 1981)

Sheri L. Dew

Our Father knew exactly what He was doing when He created us. He made us enough alike to love each other, but enough different that we would need to unite our strengths and stewardships to create a whole. Neither man nor woman is perfect or complete without the other. Thus, no marriage or family [. . .] is likely to reach its full potential until husbands and wives [. . .] work together in unity of purpose, respecting and relying upon each other's strengths. ("It Is Not Good for Man or Woman to Be Alone," *Ensign*, Nov. 2001)

MEDITATION 53

PONDER AND DISCUSS:

- What does "helpmeet" mean to you? What is one thing you can do this week to be a better helpmeet?

- Why might we be counseled to labor with each other?

- What is one way that your spouse has acted well as a helpmeet in the past?

- When have you and your spouse labored together, respecting and relying upon each other's strengths?

- How might you and your spouse unite your strengths and stewardships as you labor together this week?

MEDITATION 53

Counsel Together Regularly

M. Russell Ballard

> An executive family council [. . .] involves only the parents. [. . .]
>
> The executive family council is also a good time for wives and husbands to talk about their personal relationships with each other. ("Family Councils," *Ensign*, May 2016)

Jean B. Bingham

> Unity is essential to the divine work we are privileged and called to do, but it doesn't just happen. It takes effort and time to really counsel together—to listen to one another, understand others' viewpoints, and share experiences—but the process results in more inspired decisions. ("United in Accomplishing God's Work," *Ensign*, May 2020)

PONDER AND DISCUSS:

- What can you do to ensure that you and your spouse hold an executive family council on a regular basis?
- What is working well in your marriage?
- What did your spouse do this week that you really appreciated?
- What have you learned recently that would improve your relationship with your spouse?
- What is your greatest need right now? Your spouse's greatest need?
- What is one thing you can do to be a blessing and a support to each other this week?

MEDITATION 54

Principles of a Successful Marriage

"The Family: A Proclamation to the World"

Happiness in family life is most likely to be achieved when founded upon the teachings of the Lord Jesus Christ. Successful marriages and families are established and maintained on principles of faith, prayer, repentance, forgiveness, respect, love, compassion, work, and wholesome recreational activities.

PONDER AND DISCUSS:

- What is your vision of a successful marriage?

- What can you do to move closer to that vision?

- How can you better incorporate the principles of a successful marriage into your lives? Which principle will you focus on first?

- Why is it important to regularly schedule dates and participate in wholesome recreational activities with your spouse?

- How might sexual intimacy be a wholesome recreational activity for you and your spouse?

MEDITATION 55

There Could Not Be a Happier People

4 Nephi 1:11, 15–18

And they were married, and given in marriage, and were blessed according to the multitude of the promises which the Lord had made unto them. [. . .]

And it came to pass that there was no contention in the land, because of the love of God which did dwell in the hearts of the people.

And there were no envyings, nor strifes, nor tumults, nor whoredoms, nor lyings, nor murders, nor any manner of lasciviousness; and surely there could not be a happier people among all the people who had been created by the hand of God.

There were no robbers, nor murderers, neither were there Lamanites, nor any manner of -ites; but they were in one, the children of Christ, and heirs to the kingdom of God.

And how blessed were they! For the Lord did bless them in all their doings; yea, even they were blessed and prospered until an hundred and ten years had passed away; and the first generation from Christ had passed away, and there was no contention in all the land.

PONDER AND DISCUSS:

— After Christ had visited the Nephites following his resurrection, His influence had such a profound effect upon the people that there was no contention in the land for over a century. How might this have been achieved?

— What are some things you can do in your marriage to follow the example of the Nephites who lived without contention?

MEDITATION 56

- Nephite husbands and wives were "blessed according to the multitude of the promises which the Lord had made unto them." What might some of those promises have been?

- Has there been a time recently when the love of God dwelled in your heart and expanded your love for your spouse?

- What is one thing you and your spouse can do to be more like the happiest people who had been created by the hand of God?

NOTES _____

_____

_____

_____

_____

_____

_____

_____

MEDITATION 56

The Marriage Metaphor

Isaiah 54:5

For thy Maker is thine husband; the Lord of hosts is his name; and thy Redeemer the Holy One of Israel; The God of the whole earth shall he be called.

Ephesians 5:23, 30–33

For the husband is the head of the wife, even as Christ is the head of the church: and he is the saviour of the body. [. . .]

For we are members of his body, of his flesh, and of his bones.

For this cause shall a man leave his father and mother, and shall be joined unto his wife, and they two shall be one flesh.

This is a great mystery: but I speak concerning Christ and the church.

Nevertheless let every one of you in particular so love his wife even as himself; and the wife see that she reverence her husband.

Richard K. Hart

The marriage metaphor testifies of the great love the Savior feels for all mankind and of the blessings that await those who accept his invitation to become his spiritual sons and daughters. [. . .]

The basis for Jesus' claim that he had purchased us with His suffering is evidence that he wanted us with him for his happiness. This is an insight into the statement that Jesus is a Bridegroom and the Church is like his bride, who he takes with him back into the presence of the Father. ("The Marriage Metaphor," *Ensign*, Jan. 1995)

MEDITATION 57

Robert L. Millet

Thus He who loved us first (1 John 4:10, 19) reaches out to the lost and fallen, to the disinherited, and proposes a marriage. The Infinite One joins with the finite, the Finished with the unfinished, the Whole with the partial, in short, the Perfect with the imperfect. Through covenant with Christ and thus union with the Bridegroom, we place ourselves in a condition to become fully formed, whole, finished—to become perfect in Christ. (See Book of Mormon, Moroni 10:32.) (*The Mormon Faith: A New Look at Christianity* [Salt Lake City: Deseret Book Company, 1998], 71)

PONDER AND DISCUSS:

- In using the imagery of marriage, bride, and bridegroom, how would you describe how the Lord feels about you? How would you describe the relationship the Lord desires to have with you?

- How does the example of Christ as the faithful Bridegroom elevate your feelings and desires for your spouse?

- How might His example as the faithful Bridegroom inspire you to enhance your marriage?

- How might becoming one in your marriage help you to become fully formed, whole, finished—even one with Christ?

MEDITATION 57

Love Is a Fragile Thing

Jeffrey R. Holland

True love blooms when we care more about another person than we care about ourselves. That is Christ's great atoning example for us, and it ought to be more evident in the kindness we show, the respect we give, and the selflessness and courtesy we employ in our personal relationships.

Love is a fragile thing, and some elements in life can try to break it. Much damage can be done if we are not in tender hands, caring hands. To give ourselves totally to another person, as we do in marriage, is the most trusting step we take in any human relationship. It is a real act of faith—faith all of us must be willing to exercise. If we do it right, we end up sharing everything—all our hopes, all our fears, all our dreams, all our weaknesses, and all our joys—with another person.

No serious courtship or engagement or marriage is worth the name if we do not fully invest *all* that we have in it and in so doing trust ourselves totally to the one we love. You cannot succeed in love if you keep one foot out on the bank for safety's sake. The very nature of the endeavor requires that you hold on to each other as tightly as you can and jump in the pool together. In that spirit, and in the spirit of Mormon's plea for pure love, I want to impress upon you the vulnerability and delicacy of your partner's future as it is placed in your hands for safekeeping—male and female, it works both ways. [. . .]

[. . .] Life is tough enough without having the person who is supposed to love you leading the assault on your self-esteem, your sense of dignity, your confidence, and your joy. In this person's care you deserve to feel physically safe and emotionally secure. ("How Do I Love Thee?" [Brigham Young University devotional, Feb. 15, 2000], 3–4, speeches.byu.edu)

MEDITATION 58

PONDER AND DISCUSS:

- If love is a fragile thing, what are you doing in your marriage to nourish and protect it? What is one thing you would like your spouse to do to nourish and protect your love?

- What are some ways your spouse has tenderly cared for your hopes, fears, dreams, weaknesses, joys, or sorrows?

- Elder Holland describes marriage as the most trusting step we take. What would it look like to you to trust yourself totally to the one you love, to give yourself totally, to share your everything? What are you doing to maintain the trust your spouse has placed in you?

- If the trust in your marriage has been eroded, what can you do to help rebuild it? What can your spouse do to help rebuild it?

- What is one thing your spouse can do to help you feel physically safe? Emotionally secure?

MEDITATION 58

When Troubles Come

Bruce C. Hafen

When troubles come, the parties to a *contractual* marriage seek happiness by walking away. They marry to obtain benefits and will stay only as long as they're receiving what they bargained for. But when troubles come to a *covenant* marriage, the husband and wife work them through. They marry to give and to grow, bound by covenants to each other, to the community, and to God. *Contract* companions each give 50 percent; *covenant* companions each give 100 percent. [. . .]

[. . .] Christ's life is the story of giving the Atonement. The life of Adam and Eve is the story of receiving the Atonement, which empowered them to overcome their separation from God and all opposition until they were eternally "at one," with the Lord, and with each other. [. . .]

[. . .] Our deepest God-given instinct is to run to the arms of those who need us and sustain us. ("Covenant Marriage," *Ensign*, Nov. 1996)

Mosiah 18:8–9, 21

And now, as ye are desirous to come into the fold of God, and to be called his people, and are willing to bear one another's burdens, that they may be light;

Yea, and are willing to mourn with those that mourn; yea, and comfort those that stand in need of comfort [. . .]

And he commanded them that there should be no contention one with another, but that they should look forward with one eye, having one faith and one baptism, having their hearts knit together in unity and in love one towards another.

MEDITATION 59

PONDER AND DISCUSS:

- When adversity and afflictions come, why might some couples grow distant or walk away from each other while other couples grow closer and run into each other's arms?

- How might spouses better cling to each other when trials and troubles come their way?

- How has mourning with each other, comforting each other, or bearing one another's burdens helped you to give and to grow, to deepen your intimate connections, and to knit your hearts together in unity and love?

- Why might it be difficult to be "at one" emotionally and/or sexually with your spouse when troubles come? How might you overcome this difficulty?

- What is one thing you would like your spouse to do to support and connect with you better during times of challenge and uncertainty?

MEDITATION 59

Continue Searching for Truth

Wendy Watson Nelson

Truths about love and marriage are brought to you by the Holy Ghost from our Heavenly Father. He decreed marriage to be an irreplaceable component of His plan of happiness. The Spirit is the messenger of these truths. I urge you to seek to understand them. ("Love and Marriage" [worldwide devotional for young adults, Jan. 8, 2017], churchofjesuschrist.org/broadcasts)

Matthew 7:7–8

Ask, and it shall be given you; seek, and ye shall find; knock, and it shall be opened unto you:

For every one that asketh receiveth; and he that seeketh findeth; and to him that knocketh it shall be opened.

2 Nephi 28:30

For behold, thus saith the Lord God: I will give unto the children of men line upon line, precept upon precept, here a little and there a little; and blessed are those who hearken unto my precepts, and lend an ear unto my counsel, for they shall learn wisdom; for unto him that receiveth I will give more; and from them that shall say, We have enough, from them shall be taken away even that which they have.

MEDITATION 60

PONDER AND DISCUSS:

- How can you gain and apply more knowledge to strengthen your marriage?

- Why might married couples need to continually learn about sexual expression as their relationship matures?

- How can misunderstandings and falsehoods about sexuality affect a married couple's relationship?

- How can you be more open to receiving inspiration and counsel to enrich your marriage and your intimacy?

- What are some questions that you and your spouse would like to study and ponder together?

MEDITATION 60

What will happen as you more intentionally hear, hearken, and heed what the Savior has said and what He is saying now through His prophets? […] I promise miracles in your marriage.

—**President Russell M. Nelson**

About the Authors

Jennilyn and Dave Young enjoy being close, making each other smile, and deepening their love a little more each day. Even after twenty-nine years of marriage, they are still finding meaningful ways to become of one heart, one mind, and one flesh. Their new book, *Meditations for Marital Intimacy*, is a compilation of counsel from leaders of The Church of Jesus Christ of Latter-day Saints and scriptures, with questions to ponder, discuss, and apply. A lifelong love of learning has led them to the blessed unexpected of homeschooling their four children, connecting regularly with their extended family and book group friends, and discovering how to love each other better. Some of their favorite memories include a family home evening helicopter ride, live performances in their home theater, band gigs, music video production, cozy cabin conversations, books on beaches and in bed, hikes in the mountains of Utah, and card games at the kitchen table. Jennilyn is passionate about the word of God, education, health, and nutrition. Dave is passionate about music and Jennilyn. They aspire to create a beautiful connection daily and invite you to connect with them on Facebook and Instagram @JennilynandDaveYoung.

NOTES

NOTES

NOTES

NOTES

NOTES

NOTES

NOTES

NOTES

NOTES